REUNION

Other books by Fleda Brown:

The Women Who Loved Elvis All Their Lives
Breathing In, Breathing Out
*The Devil's Child**
*The Earliest House**
*Do Not Peel the Birches**
*Fishing With Blood**
*Critical Essays on D. H. Lawrence**

*as Fleda Brown Jackson

Fleda Brown

REUNION

The University of Wisconsin Press

The University of Wisconsin Press
1930 Monroe Street
Madison, Wisconsin 53711

www.wisc.edu/wisconsinpress/

3 Henrietta Street
London WC2E 8LU, England

Library of Congress Cataloging-in-Publication Data

Jackson, Fleda Brown, 1944–
  Reunion / Fleda Brown.
     p. cm. — (The Felix Pollak prize in poetry)
  ISBN 0-299-22180-6 (alk. paper)
  ISBN 0-299-22184-9 (pbk. : alk. paper)
  I. Title.
  PS3560.A21534R48<3M>2007
  811'.54—dc22<3M>2006031482

for my sister Melinda

Surely you never have dreamed the incredible depths were prologue and
epilogue merely
To the surface play in the sun, the instant of life, what is called life? I fancy
That *silence is the thing, this noise a found word for it. . . .*
Robinson Jeffers, "The Treasure"

The man pulling radishes
pointed the way
with a radish.
Issa

Contents

Acknowledgments

Thanks to the following periodicals in which these poems first appeared, sometimes in different versions:

Arts and Letters, "Light," "Small Boys Fishing Under the Bridge," "Knife"

Cortland Review, "Twelfth Wedding Anniversary Poem," "Elegy for a Woman Killed by a Deer on New London Road"

Florida Review, "Elegy for Donna"

Georgia Review, "Knot Tying Lessons: The Perfection Knot," "Knot Tying Lessons: The Slip Knot," "Knot Tying Lessons: The Clove Hitch"

Image, "Ode to the Buffman Brothers," "Poverty of Spirit"

Kenyon Review, "No Heron"

Lake Effect, "The Explanation"

Midwest Quarterly, "Red Paint"

Paterson Review, "Mouse"

Poet Lore, "The Death of Cleone," "What It Was Like"

Poetry, "Jack in the Pulpit," "Bladder Campion," "Canada Anemone"

Prairie Schooner, "Delaware"

Runes, "I Return to Fayetteville after Twenty Years"

Snakebird: Thirty Years of Anhinga Poets, "Reading Poetry at the Horse Meadow Senior Center"

Southern Poetry Review, "Indian River Inlet, II," "Trillium"

Southern Review, "Indian River Inlet, I," "Through Security," "Makeup Regimen"

Tampa Review, "Flying Ants"

West Branch, "If Names Started Coming Loose"

This book would be much the worse without the fiercely accurate eye of Dabney Stuart, accompanied by his endless generosity and friendship through the process of preparing the manuscript—and by the example of his own poems. I wish also especially to thank Sydney Lea, especially for his friendship and encouragement, and for his own poems, which have been models for me for years. I am grateful to the University of Delaware for a sabbatical leave that enabled me to write many of the poems in this book, and to the English Department writing faculty—Jeanne Murray Walker, Cruce Stark, Bernie Kaplan, and Gibbons Ruark—for their twenty-seven years of colleagueship and support. I also want to thank Anne Colwell for her help with "Knife," and to mention my valuable association with many other Delaware poets in writing retreats, workshops, and festivals over the last few years. Their energy and devotion to the craft have helped me more than they know. And Laura Scanlan, Director of Delaware Division of the Arts, has been helpful to me in myriad ways. Finally, I am thankful for my large family, whose love and energy keep me going. And particularly, as always, I am grateful to my husband, Jerry, for his love and friendship, and for his willing reading of everything, in every draft.

I

Canada Anemone

I count nineteen white blossoms
      which would not be
            visible except for
their wiry stems that catapult them
      above the grass like
            the last white pop
of fireworks, a toothed blast
      of leaf below. It's
            the Fourth of July
on the bank of Hinkson Creek
      fifty years ago, the powder-
            bitterness, the red
combustion, my life, since
      anemos means wind, means
            change, no matter
that I've been held all along in this
      thin twenty miles of atmosphere.
            The wind's disturbed
the leaves, rolled the waves,
      convincing enough. Each
            star of a bloom
is driven upward almost against
      its small nature. All it can do
            is hang on and die.
Still, it did want to go
      as high as possible,
            for some reason,
to sway up there like an art object.

I Return to Fayetteville after Twenty Years

The Methodist church still chimes its electric
hymns. I'm still in junior high study hall,
desk bolted to the floor. I've grown so tall,
though, that I hover over myself, where
I'm scratching a crude house on the desktop
with a straightened paper clip. It's a long way
down to the house, the one on Whitham Street,
with the creek and the crazy ironing lady
and the field and the chloroformed kittens
and the crying. Or the one on Maxwell Drive
with the crawl space and the mother cat
and the gun and the other crying,
and the impatient sex wicking itself into
the sheets. Inside the house are the original
houses of my mother, my father. They fit
the space exactly, wall against wall, all
their plots and expositions, their little worlds
carved out of materials at hand. How sweetly
the gouges improve on the desktop's
varnish! How fiercely the pencil lead drives
a darkness in, for remembrance. From up here,
I lean down as if my life were a lesson
I have to teach. Look, I say to myself, that's
you in the house, crumbling shredded wheat
into the bowl. There's your mother, so alive
the hairs on her arm glisten. Listen, does she
say anything to live by? No, it's always
the chimes, and the space between
where everything else gets in.

What It Was Like

My mother dragging the vacuum cleaner like a large cockroach
room to room. My mother folded like a moth, sitting on the stoop.

She's not crying now, she sips her Pepsi through a straw. She's "mad,"
she says, as if it were only a bug in her throat. I grow alert as a deer.

I grow aware of bad local grammar, hoards at the gate. I roar off
with my friends down Dickson Street, bringing civilization to Arkansas

in someone's T-Bird. Some conglomerate picture shifting as if
underwater, not that, but a womb-thickness. I push through, assembling

as I go. I wish I could hold onto my mother's feet, very small and white,
high-arched, ticklish. Her feet only, far enough from her eyes.

Her eyes in my memory: one brown pupil off to the side, trying
to escape, the other dutiful, their hopeless drama. Don't look at them,

but at the mottled pattern of the linoleum countertop, the flared
aluminum legs of the dinette, my rage equal exactly to my love, two

pistons. You ask me what I remember: I'm halfway up Mt. Sequoyah
on the other side, gasping for breath. I turn to catch the long Ozark valley,

the glorious translucent yellow of maples. I'll call it mothering
because of the way the land and sky hold you, and at the same time

lay a hand on the back of your neck like a dangerous lover.

for Andrea Hollander Budy

Biology Lesson

Ontology recapitulates phylogeny.
I love the sound of that,
the way heredity's an automat
set on a repeat serve. Compulsory

rhyme, I'd say. I say it now,
thinking of the pit to China
we dug that summer in Dinah's
back yard. It was our upside-down

doubles we were after. I think
of us digging past lunch,
past dinner, skinny and hunched
over that yawning, impious link

to the underworld. We were like
the buck I saw yesterday
in my path that outstayed
me: concentrated, in love with might,

maybe more with fear. The hole
could go on forever, we
could come out feet
first on the other side, the soul

of us yanked like a radish by some
bathrobe-wearing, slant-eyed
devil. We would divide
from our old selves, a martyrdom.

We would be born again.
Again, we would start up
with our plan to interrupt
the plan. It would be our discipline.

6

Fayetteville Junior High

When we weren't looking,
Mr. Selby married Miss Lewis.
We tried to think of it, tip-
toed Mr. Selby, twirling
the edges of blackboard numbers
like the sweet-pea tendrils
of his hair, all his calculations
secretly yearning away
from algebra, toward Miss Lewis,
legs like stone pillars in the slick
cave of the locker room,
checking off the showered,
the breasted, flat-chested.

       All this: another world
we never dreamed of inside
the bells, the changing
of classes: Selby and Lewis,
emerging from rooms 4 and 16,
holding hands like prisoners
seeing the sky after all those
years. "Bertha," he says. "Travis,"
she says. The drawbridge
of the hypotenuse opens,
the free-throw line slides
forward, worn floor creaking.
In homeroom, the smell
of humans, rank, sprouting,
yet this hope for us all.

Elegy for Donna

We'd meet at the top of Garland Street to slam tennis balls,
chase them like crazed pigeons. As soon as summer began
its tremble, we'd start for the pool, maybe fifteen blocks to go.

I want to live in the present there without a trace of memory.
I want to head uphill into our longings again, to feel their heat,
like heat from the sidewalks, its visible streamers.

The sidewalk bumps and curves, tree roots turn
and vanish, leaves thicken. Sweat breaks out; we're walking as if
we have forever, as if our destiny is not to die but to cross

Maple Street, to get to the pool, the chemical blue, the dank
locker room. I would like to dive in again, get my body
clear, open my eyes to the silvered upper world. But this is

all grown-up talk, thinking I know something now, when
it's only me, still, at the edge of the future as always, slap-
footing around its rim, the whole space of it rippled

and inner. Meanwhile, there was the afternoon, with fudgecicles.
What did we talk about? Math and English and boys, but
it might have been code for some divergence, some slight

inconsistency begun that brought me here, her to Rochester,
to die ten years ago today. Or what did we not say, that wedged
between us walking home in our swimsuits, shirts tied

at the waist? What happiness was that, what shiver?

The Explanation

You could say it was because she wrote
Mrs. James Lee so many times in study hall
that the name spilled outward and caught her
in its rings. You could trace the family history
of loneliness that took her hand because
she was next, or her actual fever the fall of '62,
so severe her father carried her, delirious,
pajamas and all, to the bathtub and sat her in
as she cursed him and her new town and all
that kept her from love, which had become
embodied for her already, at 17. (She had sent
her love a photo of herself, smiling, in front
of the grapevine, with the caption, "Grapes
are a sign of fertility.") And so he came
and they bought the rings and they had
the ceremony as if they were grown,
and drove to Mountain Home
for a honeymoon.

       But for God's sake
I think it's time now after all these years
to leave them alone in their black and white
Chevy, to cut loose the clang of explanations.
He's steering and smoking with one hand,
the other arm around her. She's wearing
her new white polyester blouse. He's driving
his first car, two weeks old, his sunglasses
clipped over Buddy Holly frames. They're only
going from one state to the next, but the land
spreads out, tractors and gas stations oblivious,
contented. She lights a Tareyton, two years
before the worst is known about that.
She folds her new clothes again in her mind,

each one, including her first and only negligee,
for that other newness, which really is,
for them, because they've waited for this
moment, in which she is Doris Day and he is,
well, someone, and afterward they drink a beer
and watch "Cheaper By the Dozen."

You could call it escape, all of it, playing.
You could slip and say "mistake" instead of
"escape." You couldn't know how straight
toward their lives they were driving, barely
a whisper in the other direction.

Knot Tying Lessons: The Slip Knot

The most useful temporary knot or noose.

What can I say? I turned a corner. No matter
that I doubled back, there was still progress. I was lying
low, crossing under both my coming and going,
and when I rose to see where I was, felt the cool
air on my face, I skidded like a skater, wrapped around
myself again, burrowing back up through the small
figure-eight I'd made of myself. How secure it all seemed,
how sure to result in something unfaltering—patriotic,
even. But the way things have gone, I'm left with
a looseness through the center.
There's been this tendency to let things drop.
It's the opposites I have trouble with,
the way my attention begins expanding as if
the richness has eased past the borders, no longer
lives in this constriction, this lump in my throat.
I drew you to me with such firmness, you were sure
of the implications. The exact point at which I began
to be disappointed, who knows? The more I gave myself
room to work it out, the more I felt the movement
of possibilities within me. I should have felt relieved
when all fell through, but I only felt what I am,
how I'm made. "Open your mouth," my mother used to
say, coming at me with a bar of soap because of some
word I'd said. I opened, as I do now, willing to take
the bitterness, to have done what I did.

Makeup Regimen

I've developed complicated pores, I need radiance, more beauty steps,
more ice-colored bottles, the old me exfoliated so the young one can emerge

dewy, daily. As if I could see my own face, as if the mirror reflected me
by the shortest route instead of at crazy angles, all probabilities adding up

to my face, as if it weren't our ignorance that makes things appear in their
classical forms. When the Newtonian God went away, what took His place

acts more like rain, mist, sunshine, bounded by horizons du jour. Enter
clarifying lotion, like the crisp, high range of stars. The face of night's

supposed to be naked and spread from ear to ear, but at dawn the workmen
arrive with their electric saws, their hydraulic hammers; everything's to be

built again. The sum of it is complex: for example, my mother's mouth
in her coffin was all wrong. They made her look mature, confident.

Their mistake was concentrating on the flesh, trying to fill the emptiness
with it. She had her red suit on. They took her jewelry off when all we asked

for was her ring, leaving her not quite put together forever. I like to think,
though, that dying is like falling all the way back to where everything's

held to itself by memory. Two old men I knew in Arkansas would pass
each other Mondays on their country road, driving so slowly they had time

to ask after each other's family. "Mr. Caid," one would say, and nod.
"Mr. Kimball," the other would say, and nod. The main thing was to come

along looking as much as possible like somebody same as the week before.

Delaware

An old Candid Camera skit: two men
stop cars at the border. "Delaware's closed
today," they say, and the drivers docilely turn away.

That's me, I'd be still driving around looking.
The way you ought to find a state is, things
change. Fields, then you get to a difference

that stays different, not this compass arc carved
out of Pennsylvania, this right angle drawn away
from Maryland. On a map, its name drifts

in the Atlantic, neither here nor there. It lies
inward like a cove on a creek, twigs and leaves
swirled in, and sludge, and a faint orange ring

you know is pollution, and then in a hard rain
it all moves on and starts again: cancer
slipping boundaries—highest breast cancer rate

in the country, no one takes the blame, everyone's
from somewhere else, like New Jersey, the other side
of the hypotenuse across the bay. In the middle,

Salem Power Plant steams upward, refuses
to take sides. In the south, the long slow marshes,
cypresses, snow geese, herons. Good and evil

cancel each other out—Dela*where?*—
the way the ocean tries to cancel out the shore,
and the shore walks inland and forgets itself in relation

to anything else. I don't know where I live.
You need a breath between states, to be sure
the next one's coming. "Welcome to Oklahoma,

to Missouri," for instance. I remember Arkansas that way,
as being *not those other states.* There have
to be limits, skin and bones. The poetic version

of home can open the mind like a trick-
or-treat bag and endlessly drop things in: Wilmington,
Newark, Middletown, Smyrna, Lewes, Rehoboth,

names our children learn, meaning their own
caches of grief and joy, the resonances
their ears have collected by now. But me, did I

mention I'm starting to lose my hearing? Words
grow softer, doing tricks and transformations.
I could be in a hotel room, soft clicks

in the hallway, a rumble. I can't remember the number
on the door, the sheets are empty pages. I try
to identify boundaries, as the Buddha says, separate

the strands of experience until there is no self, while
the self is full with the moment, riding the waves
of its own impermanence. I've said farewell, God knows,

many times. The day we left Fayetteville, the three
neighbor children lined up on the sad little mound
of grass to wave goodbye to our son. It was summer,

and the sun took everything out of my eyes
and kept moving. Like a fool, I've believed, though,
in each place. The little creek behind our house

runs clear, now rusty, now clear. Who or what
causes this I do not know. Runoff from lawns,
I'd guess, growing feathery weeds underwater, here,

then gone. Still, there are minnows. And you, my
utterly specific one, and our children, and our
children's children, ringing and crashing like deer

to our salt lick, appearing in the morning mist as if
through holes in the universe—their innocence
and light—leaving small berries of scat, and tracks.

The Death of Cleone

                                    Of course she mistook
her son for her husband, since
it was the lake, and summer,
and she had grown small and turning,
as if the world were a kaleidoscope and she
its center made only of mirrors.
It was his voice, his hair, his height, so she
let down her own white hair and set her lips
on his before he realized. Still, when he
held her hand at the end, he was willing to be
anyone, and he talked to her of Central Lake
again, and when he reached the edge
of words, he took her arms
and made a motion of paddling
the canoe, and she did open her eyes
across the small craft of her bed, gliding
out into the last sliver of sun.
She passed the dam at Bellaire, through
Clam River, Grand Traverse Bay,
Lake Michigan, into the dream-soup
of details, of J-strokes. It was hard work
against the drag of water, before she
remembered she was a gull, and the water
turned to air. No, not a gull. Not that far
to go. Only back to Central Lake; she was
one of the ducks lifting off, pulling up
their landing gear in their awkward
duck-flurry of voices, and it didn't matter
which one she was, or who it was that
loved her, all of them winging around
within the hollow of the lake.
So began the silence, the evening,
the turning stars.

II

Trillium

Named for its trinity of leaves, of petals.

The universe prefers
      odd numbers. It leans,
          obsessed with
what's next. It likes syllogisms,
      the arguments of
          sonnets: if A
equals B, then C.
      The ground-level
          common denominator,
the blood-red whorl
      at the base, is not
          an answer but
a turning. Does that leave you
      dizzy? What can I
          say that would
reassure either of us? Even
      our prayers have to
          catch hold
as if we grabbed a spoke of
      a merry-go-round and tried
          to convince
the universe of what we want
      stopped, reversed.
          What it gives us
instead: this bad-smelling
      beautiful bloom.
          "Let go, let go,"
is what it says, and who wants
      to hear that?

If Names Started Coming Loose

Cow, for instance, might hook itself
like a horseshoe around a fencepost.
Chair might land on a cat, try to
assimilate. *Chickadee* could shudder
loose, to discover itself staid, roomy,
with a two-car garage. The ones
left behind? Vaporous, probably
afraid, not yet knowing how to live
inside discontinuities. Meanwhile,
cow would quite naturally be grafting
itself as efficiently as possible to
the fencepost, upright, unflinching,
drawing no flies. Like the rest of us,
it would be willing to go for a small part
of the truth, a little more onomatopoeia,
a little less floating. Try to think of it:
your name, the one you've repeatedly
handed out to strangers, now landed,
say, onto the huge steel patio grill.
"I'll just throw these burgers on the
Maryann," someone might say. And you
would be moving like a rumor among
named objects, not unnoticed entirely,
but treated with the maneuvering
of the other guests who know they
must know you, but can't quite
recall . . . Makes you want to hang on,
doesn't it? It does me. To admit to myths,
vow beliefs you never thought you'd
settle for. That's the part of you that
wants to live inside mere obedience
forever, place the salad fork on the outside,

pass the potatoes clockwise. But then,
suppose there's the lightness beginning
to come on, incredible continents
inside you, rising and breaking apart,
the voice you never knew was yours.
Suppose it's so good it has no name.

Small Boys Fishing under the Bridge

1

I watch them try and try for nothing
but tiny bluegill, sunfish, crawdads even,
anything to feel a tug, though they'd call it
necessity, as if they had to feed a dozen mouths.
They bend over the night crawlers
with a whopping knife, too jagged, in love
with tools, machines, reels.
They're serious, removed, all of them,
threading half-worms as bravely as they can,
leaving me out of it, trying to act as if
the oozing is normal, required, after all
they've been taught about kindness.

2

It's excitement and mystery under here,
a boat churning through, echoing against
the bridge, and Zach, pulling up his bluegill
at last, shining and flapping.
He stops its fins down with his fist.
The fish looks at him, one eye at a time,
from its other world. From this one, the meaning
seems clear: the yanked hook, the yellow
plastic live well barely wide enough for a fish.
But there's the human to figure in,
the complications of its mind, as it crouches
beside in splashed and sticky shorts.

3

After the hammer-blow, it's not so hard
to scrape scales into a universe of stars,
to saw off the head, fish-quivers
giving way to plain flesh.
What lesson can be learned by this?
It seems like no lesson
on the blue-willow plate—only eating
or being eaten, which turns out at last to be
a quiet exchange, nothing that could have been
helped, desire being what it is,
and fish like little knives
pointed toward it all the time.

for Josh, Zach, Noah, and Daniel

Light

I don't want to get started on such a nice night, but when I'm
standing out here and the security light's blasting from the boathouse
over the way, incessantly headed my direction
as light does across water and I can't see the stars only orange
bug-light and the nasty-wasp Jet Skis angled half out of the water
and who's going to roar off on them at night anyway and I'm
without the big dipper or the little or the entire dark past
or the crawdads under the dark, and even swimming nude
is problematical in that glow that's intended to mean I try to figure
what, *here we are in the suburbs,* maybe, *because the dark's
dangerous,* and me, I like to walk out barely seeing my feet,
just flicking on a light at the end of the dock, not to go
too far, and then when it's off I'm floating with only the upper
world breaking through in pinpricks we've given names to,
in our idleness or fear, but nothing like this tactless yowling
of light. Wouldn't you think there'd be boundaries, like when
a car drives by rocking with bass and I can't hear
myself think, wouldn't you think there'd be some respect for
people's secrets, invisible as they are, some acknowledgment
that the invisible's worth something, that I'm here, that there's a god
of some sort that picks up steam in the dark spaces, the more
dark, the more chance—so I try to turn my back to the light,
but is it awful of me now to remember Kraków, Kabul,
Monrovia, the yellow bombs in the night saying Kilroy Was Here,
to want to stand on this dock representative of my version
of history, declaring no more light, no more sight of Jet Skis
taking no risks with their noses in the air, wouldn't you think
the dark would finally get angry, at least in my lifetime,
and I could watch the retribution, the darkening, that the stars
would begin to reach earth with their clear messages, that they
would have something to say after all that distance about traveling
through their opposite, doesn't it seem reasonable that I would
want to stand on the dock and wait for them to arrive?

Red Paint

Here is my father, lying sideways on the dock
trying to scrub off blood-red marine paint.
Here are his old hands and forearms, bloody,
everything he touches, bloody. My words
are so bloody, as usual, I try not to say them.
I could be ten years old, mopping up
my brother's blood after another seizure.
My father's acting like he's ten, as usual,
smearing paint everywhere. If you knew
the history. I drive to the lumberyard
after paint thinner. "Don't move," I say.
I douse the dock with thinner, too.
"Oh, for heaven's sake," he says.
"In World War II, they used to splash red paint
on the decks to get the men used to blood."

        "Oh, well," I say, because he will die
sooner than later, because the sun is a white eye,
and I've cleaned up the dock under the willow,
because the water's sloshing, gone and permanent
in its way. Because his sailboat's sleek with red,
a missile cradled on sawhorses.

        "Merely cosmetic," my father says
about my cleaning, as if I've wasted
my life. *A body doesn't like to spill,* I think.
Not even light spills. Look at the sun, stopped
by leaves, trunks of trees. There are sorrows
like hot stones, they give birth in silence.

There is my Mother scrubbing a bathroom
in heaven, folding sheets, getting to have
her version of nice. "Mother," I say, to remind
the universe I'm here, holding back with my
bare hands what still needs holding back.

Poverty of Spirit

Tina and her gypsy women roll in
with their wagon, storm the garage in their boots, shorts,
and bleached hair. I let them take everything, cheaply
—illegally—I know it when she says
don't worry about the paint cans, she has this pit
behind her house, and the other things
she can burn. *It's the fires of Hell, dying birds,*
poisoned wells. I also regret the wood, one perfectly clear
80-year-old 4 by 6, some original
cedar siding, and other straight pieces, but they're laughing and
smoking and things are flying
out of the garage, and Tina's in the wagon like God Almighty, retying
her red bandana, arranging the past
into a party,

and then the wind blows through
the emptiness, the scent of dryness,
July and its bad habits, and I am surer than usual that I will die,
that my soul is exactly the same room it was before
it collected the skin and bones, that it will be back
to that, eventually. I get up off the bank, wipe my hands
on my jeans, kind of a prayer for forgiveness, trying for a poverty
of spirit, the right kind you choose
item by item, not letting it get out of hand
like nuclear fission.

      Old paint with dangerous, leachable
lead, now I've said it, that's the critique
of me I was looking for. And then I pick mint, and chew a few
leaves, rough and sharp, a taste that's more
than half smell, and then I sweep out dry leaves and swing the doors
shut, spin the combination lock, which is 12–0–45, not
that it matters, unless I need to check
later, to see how much nothing there is
in there, to work with.

Ode to the Buffman Brothers

Timmy's so big he's awkward as a loon on land,
　　　　but when he gets on his backhoe
　　　　　　　　and his brother Luke on his Bobcat,
you can believe we were born for machinery.
　　　　They get the big maple ready to go,
　　　　　　　　Timmy rubs the backhoe's neck
against its trunk, slowly up and down until
　　　　it begins to crack, as we all would,
　　　　　　　　and falls through a perfect tunnel
of trees, wild hair every which way, Luke
　　　　scooping it, and the smaller ones,
　　　　　　　　into the huge dump truck. Then
they really begin, Timmy with his delicate
　　　　biting and scooping, clanging the small head
　　　　　　　　down on the cement walk,
lifting a chunk to the dump truck
　　　　like a dead mouse, Luke backing
　　　　　　　　and twirling in place. They do-se-do
to the low rumble of motors. They come right
　　　　to the edge of the house's foundation,
　　　　　　　　they bite out a row
of stones around the old ice-house, they leave
　　　　a perfect cliff, you should see it,
　　　　　　　　roots exposed like the wiring
of the world, the smell of dirt and rocks and roots.
　　　　Another thing: yesterday, they said,
　　　　　　　　at six-thirty a double rainbow
landed about here. They said it was a once-
　　　　in-a-decade rainbow, and I missed it.
　　　　　　　　This is what I mean about them,
what I can't get enough of. They make me
　　　　want to start over from scratch.

Knot Tying Lessons: The Clove Hitch

An important basic knot often used to fasten sail ratlines to shrouds.

Under our house, a bed
of blacksnakes, seeping out
in waves, harmless, huge,
coldly wrapping around
themselves, working against
themselves, circling each other
under and under, then
there goes one up and under
the top: hello, hello,
goodbye, goodbye, although
Ron, who's digging
to build our retaining wall,
stomps down sweaty
as a martyr, whistling,
into the ditch they just
deserted, still licked
by imaginary tongues.
The way they move
through his mind, they
could slither out of
anything, hushed as a
thousand years, clean
along the lines of least
resistance. It's the weight
of gravity, I guess,
that puts the fear in us,
the thought of the knot
made to hold, slipping loose
at last. The very thing that
keeps Ron at it, building
something opposite,
familiar, upright, stone
on stone.

Flying Ants

They appear like spots in the eye, no explanation,
>> dozens of them, winged, huge, on cue as the sun
>>> hits the eating porch between five and six, down
the wall, not attacking exactly, but clearly bound
>> for permanence, checking out the territory. Swatting
>>> and spraying notwithstanding, they bring
their friends, feeling their way down the door,
>> a prophecy. So okay, I call the exterminator;
>>> I toss my Buddhist prohibitions as if I've never
sat on a cushion. I sincerely dislike their clever
>> hinged bodies, their fierce faces you can barely see
>>> under their flailing antennae and broad banshee
foreheads coming on like the final chapter, and what
>> can one do—that's the point—against their gut-
>>> instinct mindless as a lynch mob? I can be
having my glass of wine, evening sun striking
>> the lake at its low sparkle-angle, but my mind
>>> keeps turning corners, alert for signs
of trouble, working hard to slow the pace of things,
>> preoccupied as Jesus watching in the garden for wings,
>>> only the welcome kind. Sometimes it's so
lonely on this earth, so much I don't know.
>> Even the sky has its other side, and soon will let through
>>> only glints of what now seems true.

For My Daughter's Fortieth Birthday

*Particles that were once connected will, when separated, behave as if
still connected, regardless of the distance between them.*
John Stewart Bell

Einstein called it "spooky action at a distance."
I'm rubbing my nose, and what are you doing,
now, dear one? What parts are we putting together?

I dragged you into this. What age is like, really,
I had no idea: turns out, the present settles
into its nest of memories and likes it there, even

when it stings. Let me start over. I am walking
North Intermediate Lake Road on October 7th,
not long till your birthday, sun on spider webs—

stop signs of dew and sun, one after the other,
strung across stalks, a bloom-field of sun-charges
with their studious lines to the center. Time's

turned out to be my subject. It climbed
the ladder of my attention, spinning its internal
juices, never using itself up. It hasn't been pushy.

It's begun to feel like my best friend. Let me
start over. Memory's not as easy as I said: it muscles
horribly upwards, sometimes, bigger than I am,

carrying nasty details in its arms. I keep eating them
like a spider, so not everything will come your way.
I like to think of you where you are right now,

driving kids to school in Massachusetts.

I'm walking the lake road in Michigan, watching
leaves turn and burn in the eye of Time.

How dear it is to me, the way it holds you in its sun-
dazzled arms as you round a curve and brake
at the sign, squinting your dozen little wrinkles.

The Moon Is Moving Away

The moon is moving away from earth an inch a year.
In the old days, it was almost entirely romance and danger,

but even with our precarious tilt, we started thinking science
would win. Though without the moon, we'd wobble:

burn/freeze, burn/freeze. It's hung on, a soundless pendulum
between us and oblivion. Even after the one giant step,

the tragedies, it shines up there like a quarter,
that old image. However, even an occasional rhapsody in its favor

is largely ignored by the media. The only thing that would
get their attention is if it toppled off the edge of gravity and left us

lurching, or if the man in the moon turned out to be made of oceans
as marketable as the Caribbean.

                              Unfortunately, what romance does
is remind us of loss, which makes us sad, or makes us joust

at windmills in the name of our ideals, which is why
we keep giving it up. Romance makes me think of my mother,

who must have sat on the dock the same way I'm doing now
and looked at the moon in the water. I imagine her still beautiful,

my father still overseas. I recommend the moon on such occasions
to loosen up the tight fit of life: its childlike willingness

to reflect back our own thoughts, its apparent ease as it moves
imperceptibly toward its private fate.

No Heron

Herons are bigger than egrets, though they have the same long legs.
My father said one with an eight-foot wingspan flew over his boat.
I would like to be shadowed by something that big. It would seem

like poetry, just out of reach, moving and making a bare flush
of wings, and I would think of it long after, the way it was heading
away from me. My longing would not be satisfied even if I could

grab its scrawny legs in my hand, even if it nuzzled up to me.
I would be looking up the origin of *heron* with my free hand, and
when I read Greek, *to creak,* and Old High German, *to scream,*

I would wait for it to begin, but it would not say anything to me
in this boat which I am not in, but at my desk hoping for the heron,
a big one, as I said, so I can say, "Wow, look at that!" as if I were

getting up a circus. Out there are herons white and blue, not really
blue but smoky, with wings bigger than their bodies, dipping and
standing motionless beside lakes and rivers. Out there are universes

expanding until the space between atoms is too far to do anyone
any good. Thus, somewhere this minute one heron is calculating
the distance between his beak and a fish, the way it shifts. It is

as if he travels in space until heron and fish are swallowed into
each other. There is no heron at my desk. In fact, the absence
of heron is how I would define my study: no heron on the ceiling,

no heron on the floor, no heron on the wall, so that of course
I think of nothing but heron, how it floats its weight on one leg,
for example, flying that way even when it's not.

Knot Tying Lessons: The Perfection Knot

A favorite loop among anglers, it has survived the advent of slippery nylon monofil, which has rendered many other knots obsolete.

How do we keep from going mad,
starting over with marriages and children,
making the same mistakes?
Over and over, we leave behind
the buoys that marked the shallows
we should have seen. They bob like zeros
behind us, counting for or against, who
can be sure? Maybe everything was
simpler than we thought from the start,
perfect as the disk of the sun, and the first
loop we took was never supposed to be
tied in some frivolous bow. Maybe
we were to come through the loop bravely,
cross its outer border until we could see
clearly how it was we began all this,
slip under what we used to think
was the route, until we caught
our waywardness in a noose, and nothing
could slip loose. Maybe it's the kind of thing
you have to teach your hands to do
without puzzling too much about it,
the way you faithfully get up, go to work,
come home. Like the rotation of the planets,
you have to believe that just because
no one says so, doesn't mean you aren't
okay, more than okay, really,
in your devotion to what you can't
exactly explain.

III

Bladder Campion

They come in airy flotillas
        on each stem, little flower-
            blimps, propellers
of petals at their back ends,
        which makes me think
            how heavy with history
we are, and how alone, thus forgivably
        prone to personification
            of the gods.
We imagine the little bladders puffing
        themselves out because of
            their excellent
and homeopathic ideas, the barely
        earthbound kind that no one
            takes seriously
until they save the world.
        Every story we tell is only
            Horatio Alger, a pale,
yellowish, and ordinary boy
        at the end of the row
            in junior high, who finally
amounts to something. A surprise,
        a profusion of campion,
            to demonstrate that
after the guns, the tanks,
        the barbed wire we wanted
            so desperately to avoid
in our story, blooms will spread
        back across like plain,
            kind words.

Perspective Map

Looking at Richard Edes Harrison's perspective map, "Southeast to Asia," originally published as "Southeast to Armageddon" in the March 1942 issue of Fortune *magazine.*

You'd never suspect a thing,
dotted borders, spider veins of highways,
the earth curved as an eyeball from up here.
I kissed my mother's forehead the day she died,
that's what it feels like, the height.

I like Tibet, pushed up at the edge
of India like a giant wave, which becomes
the spine of Afghanistan, Iran, down to Turkey.
It's hard to say "gunfire," or "mutilated bodies,"
with those orange wrinkles blooming

like marigolds, those lighter plains
with the sprawled lettering, the Tigris and Euphrates
forming a violin on their way to the Persian Gulf.
Still, it's hard to miss the oil rigs tethered
where they meet, the double bowstring

of the pipeline from Kirkuk almost to Amman.
From up here, though, it could be a craze line
in porcelain, or roots. The space between here
and there is sheer, my body an ark
on the sea of it. I could go on forever, except

I can almost feel it coming on, the startled presence,
winged, with the troublesome branch in its bill.

Mouse

I admire the way mouse dashes across the top bracket
of the blinds while we're reading in bed. I admire the tiny whip

of its tail at the exact second my husband tries to grab it.
I admire the way it disappears into our house and shreds various

elements. I admire the way it selects the secret corridors
behind cupboards and drawers, the way it remains on the reverse

side of our lives. The mouse is what I think of when I think of
a poem, or of music, going straight for the goods, around

the barrier of our thoughts. It leaves droppings, pretending to be
not entirely substantial, falling apart a little here and there.

Clearly, it has evolved perfect attention to detail. I wish it would
concentrate on the morning news, pass the dreadfulness out

in little pellets. Yesterday I found a nest of toilet paper and
thought I'd like to climb onto that frayed little cloud. I would like

to become the disciple of that mouse and sing "Wooly Bully"
in a tiny little voice in the middle of the night while the dangerous

political machines are all asleep. I would like to have a tail
for an antenna. But, I thought, also, how it must be to live alone

among the canyons of cabinets, to pay that price, to look foolish
and trembling in daylight. Who would willingly choose to be

the small persistent difficulty? So I put out a spoonful of peanut butter
for the mouse, and the morning felt more decent, the government

more fair. I put on my jeans and black shirt, trying not to make
mistakes yet, because it seemed like a miracle that anyone tries at all.

Birthday

Speaking of mortality: over the inlet yesterday,
two air-show planes clipped wings.
One dove into the sea, pilot drowned—another
loss in the recent sea of them, as particular

as the rest, people leaning on the railings, watching
out for hours the way we do when
to turn away would seem to be
forgetting. Today's my birthday. I take the kids

to Bachmann's, buy them what they want—
Styrofoam planes—and walk them
to the field. Jake's wide-winged 747 scribes
a mighty arc around the apple tree, half-free

of us—one flight out of four. It has to be positioned
right, wings slid forward in the slot,
ailerons—if you can call the slight flaps
that—bent down. We're giddy

with the odds for tragedy. Samantha's picked
a smaller plane, its wings too short, fuselage
too fat. It spirals down and slams, nose first, nearly
every time. She's crying. It's my

birthday. The whole idea was happiness.
"Guess what?" I say. "The spaceship Apollo
landed on the moon exactly on my birthday, 1969."
I don't say it was only dust

and rock up there. I lie on my back
in the grass, feet up, balance Sam on her stomach
and swing her back and forth until she's
laughing, nothing to do with proportion, only

to do with the delicate sky, and resistance, and drag,
and wind-sheer, the grand design that settles
the horizon down around us.

for Jacob and Samantha

Twelfth Wedding Anniversary Poem

I've lasted three days longer now than marriage number two,
a week longer than my number one. But the twenty-three years you

shared with your previous darling—I have a ways to go. Still,
we have to account for the way time compresses, distills.

We've been together barely nineteen percent of your life,
now, twenty percent of mine. All that wake behind us, that strife,

it's as if we're wading through peanut butter. Neither of us
keeps souvenirs, other than our children, but every time you touch

my elbow, the inside of my wrist, I think of the difference. Not
think. The undertow of the past sounds a tone against that spot

like a temple bell under my skin. We're never entirely alone.
Let me put it this way: suppose we go to the matinee, our known

life left out there in the sun. We're ready to fling ourselves into
the plot, shed a few tears, which is the fun of it. Something new.

Then we're stunned by the inside light, made of all our infinite
remembered people and places, reshuffled to form this exquisite,

this strange tale. Sure, it makes us sad, or sorry, but the edifice
itself is pure bliss: all of us here, we're all caught up in the kiss.

Wild Lily of the Valley

Among the ordinary lilies
      of the valley, their bells
            lined up neat
as choristers, you're the country
      cousin, tiniest sparkler
            of bloom, stamen
projecting, nothing shy about
      you. And who isn't sexy
            under the trees
by the lake, who isn't
      a little aggressive,
            full of the need
to ignore the rules, to say
      something directly
            out of the thunder
of ground, the whole dark
      that spawned us?
            Nothing greater
than sex. The dark would run on
      forever without it.
            You show up
with your frowsy equipment
      powered by two clapping
            leaves, to unbalance
the civil town. Or, it may be
      my mind taking hold,
            tangling desire
in my hair until it is all a Medusa's
      coil, something we
            come to together.

Rubbing Feet

I do love the rubbing, the putting pressure
    to bear. I love the bony, coral-like base
        from which our lives

rise democratically, their mutual aggrieved
    history, the quid pro quo, I do you,
        you do me,

the more the better, better than sex, the way
    it goes on and on as the mystery
        we are to each other

and to ourselves works itself gradually, mutely,
    closer to the surface. I'm cheered by
        the way we take hold

of the separate, colder regions, the ten brave
    peninsulas, as if it were possible
        to speak words of hope

directly through them upward to the mainland.
    It's all a particular, terrible,
        blunt attention.

I remember the two old women in heavy coats
    at the corner of 49th and Broadway
        who kept stroking

each other's cheeks and crying while the crowd
    passed to either side as if they were
        a single black rock.

Couldn't they see how the women were praying
    for them, singing for them, how
        happy the women were?

Reading Poetry at the Horse Meadow Senior Center

We'd been told fish for lunch, so we took bets on how it would be
cooked and I guess I won, although we couldn't be sure if it was
baked or broiled under the sauce, which, being guests, we pushed
around against the spinach. Not true: some of us ate, including Syd,
who lived nearby and said don't joke, he might *be* here someday, and
we were all

scanning tables, seeing our own bodies rounding back to creation,
our exact and precious sufferings slowly leaking out. The beached
whale of poetry, I thought, not seeing Syd but myself, exhausted into
prose. Syd got up, as directed, post-scrod and pre-cobbler, so people
wouldn't drift away, and he read a poem that played up the local, and
then I pulled

the mike toward them as far as the cord went, using my old joke
about the end of my rope, and they laughed, and I started with a
poem about my daughter that seemed to end right. Then I read
"Dock" because of its repetition, so they wouldn't miss rhyme too
much, that elephant in the room. I had time between to think of
Longfellow, the way

"shining big sea waters" lies off in the varnished distance and leaves a
person free afterward to take a nap. Then I read the one about my
grandfather forgetting where he was and thought halfway through,
uh-oh, but they smiled and clapped, sure of where they were, and by
this time those who wanted it had finished a second dish of peach
cobbler

and I felt really happy, useful, part of the general flow of things. I felt
like a closing line myself, made of nothing but words intended to
swim out into the stratosphere, but caught, luckily, among the
wheelchairs and walkers.

Elegy for a Woman Killed on New London Road by a Flying Deer

As the deer hit the hood of the first car

and flew backward into her own

windshield, hoofs and fur, I hope there was

an instant when it was not just surprise,

but something important. Maybe the doomed

pass matter-of-factly from one state

to another, but I hope they note the transition

with interest, their attention for once

exact and full. She's definitely got my

attention, with the deer rocketing on,

wild nostrils, wild eyes that also know

this is it—the final event that comes fast

and slow at once. Whatever faith I have,

shattering is where it starts. I have her

feeling gorgeous for a second, her old

fictions of herself flying headlong

and light as the holy ghost into the actual

creature. I have her devoted for that second

to love, meaning certain tendencies

fulfilled. Finally, the alternations, the in

and out of breath, the eating and eliminating,

the loving and hating, meeting without

caution or shame—not in theory, but in

fur, eye, tuft of ear-hair, hoof, glass,

bone: flaring, fused.

The Student

on the re-casting of "The Student," a statue by Charles Parks in front of the Newark Free Library, Newark, Delaware

Who could tell if he's not the same,
re-cast and set back on the same pedestal,
Abe Lincoln beard roughed and aflame
with sun again, same bare Huck Finn feet

and rolled-up trousers, wrinkles burned
solidly in, firm veins? If he could see—
if he looked up he'd see the scene
slightly changed, new library turned

now toward trees and parking lot.
But he's perfectly into himself, the way
most of us are, replaced but not
lost every seven years, within

our shimmering cell-change. Maybe in his brass
heart he's glad to be starting over, but he
would like to know a lot of things,
like what he means, his deliberate mass

placed here, book upside down
on his lap, not reading but thinking about
what he's reading, or dreaming, a dreamer induced
by the reading. I feel like a thread let loose

from his thoughts: off, floating, wondering
if I'm any better after all my farewells,
my changes, than I used to be, if I wear
this body more gracefully, if anyone can tell.

The Girl Thit Got Struck with Lightning

*title of a book made by Noah, age 5, a week before
the birth of his baby sister*

Page 1: Stick-legged girl. In spite of tough arms
sprouting out of her head, and glove-hands,
lightning zips through her. Or, she could be
lightning itself, part of its yellow plan.

Page 2: Overhead, clouds soldier on.
A bad time, calling for big booms,
two on the right, two on the left, a sky
of rain-dots, and lightning.
She's been born to it, she has to
take it: eyelashes, pupils,
exclamation points of fingers.

Page 3: Sun comes out in the upper corner,
ceiling of blue sky, nothing wicked
in sight. She stands alone,
smiling, arms askew.

Page 4: "Ouch, ouch," she says.
Lightning lurks inside her dress,
sun smiling like a huge zinnia.

Page 5: Parents call, "Time for dinner,"
in front of a house. The house
grows a vine of green lightning on its side,
but that, says Noah, is The End.
People have dinner and want her
there. She hasn't been destroyed,
just poked, hard. The thin body
of the house isn't telling.

Indian River Inlet, I

March: nothing here but a blank tinkertoy city of docks,
and one revved-up loon piercing the watery center
with its sharp, ancient beak. All alone, it locks

and unlocks the depths. I remember to think how weird
for a bird to fly through water. Meanwhile, little pings,
mooring rings nudging shoulders with the pilings,

and I'm shifting foot-to-foot on the balcony, waiting
for the loon to show, wondering why it divides itself, how
it knows how. I wonder if it's mocking me.

A fishing boat comes through. Red and blue
jackets emerge, attach tough lines. Way out, dashing
along: eight wild sails. If the sea were thrashing,

we'd be saved by that exclamatory wall of posts. It's
all dangerous: water, air, these railings and thermal
doors. It's a wonder anyone leaves the womb, that we haul

our sails up into this. Notice how far I've come, though—
I want credit, here—to swing this far out between one
thing and another. It's hard, given my dumb,

uncontrollable impulse toward harbor. I like to go down
and pull the covers over, but here's the loon again, rhyme
leaps up. It's a radical world, a boat pitching around

at its lines, that one there cheerily named *Lost Time.*

For Bill, Injured in Final Dress Rehearsal

You greet us, your pound of flesh nothing but
    pounds, foot propped on pillows. You've kept
        your ratty Shylock beard,

though, repeating lines every day in case you mend.
    Cast out, smarting, a whole life prepared, only
        to let the understudy go on

with it: like divorce, someone else raising
    the children. Well, not that bad, but still. To keep
        that Jew on life-support week

after week, snorting his snorts, lifting your head
    to his arrogant pitch. Oh, the others may call him cruel,
        vindictive. "What judgment shall

I dread," you repeat, "doing no wrong? You have
    among you many a purchased slave. . . ." and so on.
        You prop Shylock up

inside your fate. You take him for a drive—
    something you can do with your good foot. You point out
        a blond kid zipping by

on his skateboard, two thin swatches of green hair
    floating backward, an Ariel come up through seaweed.
        You use him to demonstrate

our contradictory urges, the way we strain
    against mercy, that wants ease, but we need
        house lights down, curtain up.

in memory of Bill Leach

Lady's Slipper

Where are you going
        in your yellow kayak
                with your curlicue leaf-
paddles, your one red-flecked
        petal-sail? How
                will you get there
over the great fern-waves, under
        the young maples,
                the doomed elms?
I question your ability
        to survive, this close
                to the road in the
twenty-first century, but
        the apparent ease
                with which you've
arisen and blown yourself
        into translucence
                makes me think
you could go on forever,
        after all, and alone,
                making the cup
of yourself out of nothing
        but loamy woods.
                I recognize bravery
when I see it, the way it opens,
        the way it enters itself
                so that all
that remains is flower.

Oppressions

1. Arthritis

The old men climb out of
cars, considering each
rotation of ball and socket—
the workings of their bodies
recently separate,
inscrutable. They don't
wince because it would be
a long road ahead, wincing,
though they observe
with some surprise the way
pain is quietly passionate,
like an old wife. They touch
a hip, a knee, to settle down
a flame they haven't energy for,
one that calls them back
each time they start to go.

2. Hot Flashes

As the skin wears thin,
desire itself begins to burn
through, to set fire to the old
unspoken angers, the times
nobody's mentioned
since, the years that turned
away unfinished. God!
Who wouldn't melt, all
the building up, the changing,
the trying to stay the same?

Now it's got to be wrung out
of the nightgown, the sheets.
On the table, an entire
book devoted to nothing
but night, flared open,
face down.

3. Bunions

In the old neighborhood,
suffering was endured.
Whoever got in trouble,
the sighs of the mothers
were as good as forgiveness.
As if they knew a secret
subcutaneous beauty.
No one had to tell them
that if so much as a foot rubs
to ruin, the mind will begin
to toughen against it, and
one day the balance will
shift: surprised by the hard
city of its own making,
it will turn inward
against itself.

4. High Blood Pressure

How can it keep on, she asks:
same heart, same bird-
like flaps, same arteries
roaring like trees, same mad

squirrels filling holes?
Capillaries so thin blood cells
travel single file. She imagines
the fragile exchange, CO_2
fighting back to the heart, the
lungs. The nuclear plants
steaming, the fields of guns
crammed with ambition. When
she gets this way, he slides
his hand down her back
to demonstrate again love
floating like a raft.

Through Security

I take off my boots because of their steel shanks.

I take out my orthotics, place my coat and purse in the bin,

place my carry-on on the belt. I take off my shirt, my jeans,

my bra. I take out my contacts. I take off my makeup

and earrings, strip the dye from my hair. I relax my stomach

to its honestly protruding shape. Still, it's all over the TVs

about me. I'm buzzed again as if there's been no progress at all

since the club-carrying, the dragging-by-the-hair. I take off

my skin, veins flying like ropes, organs dropping away

one by one. I address the additional matter of bones:

unfasten ball from socket, unhook ligaments,

leave the electronic eye no place to rest.

I am almost ready to go, if I could quit

thinking, the thinking that goes on

almost without knowing, the tiny person

crossing her legs in the back

of the mind, the one who

says, "I still love you,

dear guilty flesh."

Walker

Equally office or lounge, it allows you to fold down
its seat, set the hand brakes, and reach into its brown-
flowered Velcro-attached cotton bag for cell phone, or
pen. It's slim enough to roll between refrigerator
and door, and, with brakes, you can come to the brink
of the stairs, alone. You can pull close to the sink
and shred lettuce, and if you knock some leaves
to the floor, you can reach in your bag and retrieve
with the long-handled clamp, unless the leaves are thin
and frail, in which case someone will gather them
up later, in the silent collusion of the sick and the well,
both of you sure now what love is, the solid shell
of what may have seemed nebulous before, but which
turns out to be silence, dishrag, plate, and lettuce.
Especially for you, love has entered inanimate
objects. Between you and them exists a new intimacy.
Who wouldn't feel a little jealous? Your walker's
your little Florida, your getaway, your awkward
moves together turned to grace, the space between
here and there your common fate. When you lean
together, it doesn't look like tiredness, more a new
idea you both just had, the world turned resolute
and recent. At the window, a cardinal thrums
its song to you both, cold as aluminum.

Indian River Inlet, II

I notice angels finally fell out of fashion, after maybe ten years
of pumping up and down the ethereal plane of poems, poking
their feet through the membrane of reason. Maybe the unseen

got bored with landing behind the scenes and decided to step
plainly onstage holding a diagrammed sentence, the ribs of how
wings work. In any case, here it's only seagulls, trying to wow

space with their cries, and the hum of a solitary water pump
in the background. I don't mind growing old without angels.
By now I know the way plain vowels and consonants lump up

to push things along. Motion's always sounded like wings.
Maybe it's herald of something, maybe not. A hundred
twenty-seven posts hold up the dock out there, one by one,

so it appears to float. The shoreline across appears to float
in the bay. Whoever I am floats on the bony construction
of my body. I've never seen my face firsthand. It's kind of fun,

going through life guessing; it's the best part, actually, like
stepping off a cliff every second, never hitting bottom because
there's always one more. Like having wings, but less dignified.

IV

Jack in the Pulpit

The Jack in the Pulpit folds
      over itself like a safety pin.
           It's deep
in the woods, the hatchling
      of a dream in which
           the red-veined
and phallic manages
      to seduce you with
           the graceful curve
of vestments. You might
      like to think of it
           as a small ship
with sail unfurling
      toward a New World,
           the excitement
of discovery—yours—but
      it acts more like
           a held tongue,
because when you can't go
      anywhere, privacy
           becomes your grace.
What did Donne know,
      or Jonathan Edwards?
           The air itself curls,
and down inside, only
      a hummingbird is able
           to figure it out.

Knife

Coach Cars of Days

Is the happy part days or moments later? Earlier? Things slide
through, a Metroliner of metaphors: Thanksgiving, Christmas,
bearing up against the sudden walls, tattered flags, truck beds,
concrete pipes, corrugated brown warehouses, silted ponds with
geese. Refuse and rust, the various ball fields, one game in
progress, its flush and fuss, no reference to us. On the train to
Boston for Thanksgiving. Or, all of us at the long table with the
china, plate after plate of shining destination.

A Moment Suspended Like a Plumb Line

Over the motion of seasons, Thanksgiving and Christmas. Or like a
knife, or whatever is used to saw open your brain to go after the
tumor the size of a tangerine, caught in the crux of the optic nerves,
at the carotid artery, the pituitary. The delicacy of this requires
ignoring metaphor. Even though a person's transformed—moment,
moment, moment—the trick is in keeping track. The trick's in
staying with you like a surgeon. Who cares who our crazy father is,
our poor mother was? I help you snap the flapping green gowns,
one in front, one in back. They put your clothes in a plastic sack.

The Aesthetically Pleasing Shape of the Human Body

The lesser is to the greater as the greater is to the whole: the
Golden Section: cross, crux, crucial, crucifix. In front of St. Mary's
hospital in Saginaw, Michigan, the statue of Mary stands demure,
bronze, encouraging. But high over the main doors, she's art deco,
almost gone already, refined to memory, an aerodynamic flame.

The Unfaithfulness of the Mind

The way it keeps drifting up and down, forward and back, the sign
of the cross. Thursday, the night before, John made quattro

formaggi pizza. Pizza Giovanni, he said. This time last year you were in Florence together. It's extraordinary, all of it, the pencil point of a tumor you were born with, and now, its arrogance, assertiveness. And the breath that's traveled though a corridor so many times it believes it's entitled. As if the unimaginably vast universe could agree to keep meeting itself like this! *Corridor. Corridor* clicking along: door, door, door, a movement like the bowels, the diaphragm, carrying us.

The Speechlessness of the Sun

Rising over the fields on our way to the hospital, huge orange Midwest sun, spreading like butter along the snow-ripples. Christmas lights still on, the shapes of trees and reindeer, those night messages, even as the sun starts up again. I try to think what the messages might contribute to the general silence. Deliver me from metaphor. I can deal with the painted windows of the hospital lobby—an angel on a yellow star, dangling his feet, a pink-nosed mouse carrying a spotted Christmas ornament, a yellow-chested penguin—because of their obvious intention. The angel, the mouse, the penguin keep trying for three and a half hours as we wait to hear from surgery.

Silence As If Heard from the End of a Tunnel

At the end of the tunnel, your shocked, quivering body, curled, cut to the core, the ventilator, the mass of tubes. I know I'm living right now, complexly, many chambered. I touch your cheek, the you-and-not-you. The bruised right eye flowering, the brain seizing, trying to steady itself like a small craft. How long I have lived, finally to see how we can be ripped in a moment far from ourselves. How time can be collected into glucose bags, urine bags, potassium bags. I am touching your arm as if it were our mother's arm, or my other arm, disappearing.

The Shiftlessness of the Landscape

A couple more inches of snow. John has a tree sent, and your sons and I hang every silly ornament, trying to get them right. Your neighbors have tacked their usual obscenely pink bows on greenery. What's been withheld, the garish, begins to shine forth, unencumbered. Thanksgiving to Christmas, the year moves to finish itself, its other nature.

A Knife Passing through Butter Barely Disturbs a Thing

The molecules part, the atoms steer their flocks of electrons to either side, like mother ducks. How spacious matter is, spacious as a laugh, the way it opens the diaphragm. Here's a joke: your head wrapped in gauze, tuft of hair, tube sticking out the top. You're a cartoon sick person! The tube drains off blood: ah, an escape route from the interior. I don't know now if we could have escaped our childhood after all, even though we tried as hard as standup comedians. Here are the smiling nurses, keeping the machines occupied while you go on getting away. When we came, it was just past Thanksgiving. Now it's past New Year's, nothing between.

How Satisfying Is the Knife, How Pure

I envy the knife; it is all performance. It has no interest in the infinitely slow absorption of blood back into the brain, the wheeze of the respirator. I envy the CT scan, the slices of brain backlit on the screen in scientific portions so thin no one need feel sorry for any one of them. I envy the white areas and the gray, the way they keep their own counsel. I begin to suspect that days are a human creation, that the light and dark cancel each other out. To stand by your bed is to be nothing. Your tongue is a little bit out, your one eye a little bit open, but none of this has to do with you.

Things That Could Happen

(1) A nuclear bomb could tire of waiting. (2) Global warming could keep on melting the icecaps until a huge amount of methane gas is released that causes further warming, forming a cloud so dense as to block out the sun, causing a deep freeze. (3) High energy particle accelerators could create hyperdense "strange matter" that attracts nearby nuclei, thus growing larger until the entire planet is compressed into a sphere no more than 100 meters in diameter and rolls away under the bed like a lost nickel.

What Actually Happens

What actually happens when I speak to you, after the tiny bones of hammer, anvil, stirrup? After the internal seas, waving their 20,000 cilia? What happens after their little electric jolts to the brain? What happens when I call the family, one by one, on my cell phone? Between the word and the word, nothing but radio signals. I could be saying a poem—who knows what happens out of sight between the words? And who knows if what comes up on the other side is past or future? I could be Jonah, trying to say something from here about fear and hope, those lozenges of abstraction, among the slippery fish-belly ligaments.

Cradle of Words

Remember now in your sleep the prayers of various flavors of Christians, of Jews, of the one Muslim in the hospital lab, of Buddhists, of several atheists, in their way—the many who offered to carve for you out of the dark a bright cradle of words upon which you can be carried. *This one please carry. Carry on myth, on history. Encrust this one with our longing, with the magic longing calls its own. Saw this one in half and let her emerge whole. Through whatever narrow sleeve, let mystery fly out like a dove.*

The Cheerfulness of the Nurses

The way they raise their voices as they come in, as if they wish to reinforce the need for living. Tweakers of tubes, adjusters of clamps and pillows. They flip the urine bag, they draw blood. They say only enough to maintain for the day, one day at a time. There's the Good Cindy and the Bad Cindy. One is clear, informative, exact, the other vague, unsure. Somewhere, the physician makes his rounds. Who wouldn't like to believe he's only a few floors away, coming this way, bringing a worldview, a philosophy?

Snow

Falls, caked and heavy. Shadow, its acolyte.

The Brain Thinking of Return

Maybe it struck the brain just now, the idea of return, a kiss of electricity. Maybe the brain took a blowzy leap before it chanced losing its nerve. Or, maybe from the first breath of anesthesia, the brain's been plotting the landscape of return as strictly as a cartographer. Maybe the images the just-opened eye sees were first interior, moving outward, the difference between in and out not what we think, but easier, more porous. The eyes open, they become yours, gradually, barely, brownly, from the blank world back, tiredly taking on their work. What an effort it is to *be*, to carve a clean line through the rubble.

To Think of Latitude and Longitude at the Same Time

To place oneself deliberately in the crosshairs. To set a special table for Thanksgiving, to wash up, to decorate the tree and take it down. To light even these few fires that call attention, in the dark. *Holy Mary, snow queen, kite, flying with your flared bones over the entrance, I am having a revelation now. I imagine you making your choice. "How hard things are, already, how seasonal," you complain*

to the angel, but then you say, "Okay, sure, why not have everything?
Why not here?"

And the Form of Things Is Fallen

Onto the bed, aching, onto the wheelchair, the walker, the railings at the toilet, the sitting up wobbling against the therapist, the slow clothes on and off, as demarcations. Flight with its maddeningly invisible wings marries the lumbering form of things and agrees not to give up, never to give up on each other, agrees to go home, to live in the same house, to eat Kashi together while listening to the morning news, to complain bitterly about the government, to hope for better.

On a Marble Relief Sculpture of an Unknown Boy, 1865

Biggs Museum, Dover, Delaware

X is at a slight profile, the muscles of his pointed little chin
and lower lip pulled tight. If he had eyes instead of stone,
they'd be clear, perspicacious, resolved to rid the world

of whatever it needs ridding of. X is the kind who loves
a zero hour, a great romance. You can understand why
someone would want that in stone. It seems to say

we can all make it through the war, the subway murders,
the children lost down wells. X stands up even to the neutrinos
pouring through everything with their ghostly mass.

He remains plastered like a face transplant onto foreign
bone, holding on beyond the loss of his name, his past.
When I look at my grandson Josh who looks like me, I see

how things are endlessly replaced, something lost,
something gained: a shiver at the root, bell-strain inside
the bell. Cold pushes into my eyes. I almost remember,

I remember the noble thoughts, the way I looked into
the future, buttoned up, as if there were a war out there.
The big wars were just past, the ones coming on, private

as my own skin. I looked like this boy. How permanent
I was, how beautiful because of what I didn't know.

Bridal Veil Falls

Spread-legged, exposed, sun blasting in at ninety-three degrees,
open door required to feel the fan across the hall,
I'm half-dressed, half-asleep, in the 125-year-old room
at Pinestead Lodge where once was weaving, once looms,

once cows in the barn, once hay baled beneath the White Mountains,
now only heat trapped beneath various shingle-rotted roofs,
and me, residual, this century's product: a sedimentary press of Freud,
phonics, French, church camp, Claritin — a tabloid

of rock and roll, Doonesbury, divorces. I get up and stretch my back
like a bug on the rag-rug floor; I stretch the hamstring,
the hips, one one-thousand, two one-thousand, spreading collapsed
disks, pulling them away from each other,

from the pushing-down past that wants to wallow in itself,
trying to stop it with my set of vertical, overloaded
bones. Now, hot, restless, I head down the shimmer-road
like the Anglo-Saxon I am, baseball-hat helmet, tennis-shoe boots,

the quick, the tick of the conquering mind, hypothalamus heightened,
scouting a route out of the sun and into the trees,
through fern beds, Indian Paintbrush, buttercups, and a frieze
of unidentified star-white blooms, toward what?

Toward the dark undercover, the melodramatic chasms,
the downhill brook-singing. To head uphill against the downhill,
to get an A in climbing, to see strict Mrs. Bridenstine still!
holding up my paper, the only A in the class.

How exhaustive the mind is, inventing its absurd
tests! A stone wall melts into the earth near Franconia,
New Hampshire. That fact is stone. It can hold for years, slowly blurred
with moss and ferns, finally blurred back to the earth

from whence it arose—granite, fire-rock,
a pocket of magma trapped, cooled, risen, rounded, stacked,
sinking with dizzying speed compared to the universe, which keeps its own
slow mind turning, returning, obsessing, while I'm trying to extract

some purpose, the trail steeper now toward Bridal Veil Falls.
I meet a couple coming down, sweaty faces open, satisfied,
having made it up and mostly down against (my take on it) the tide
of Wal-Marts, McDonald's, corporate mergers,

the obese ease of America. Ahead of me, in New Hampshire,
water rises from the ravine of its own making
and falls, taking its gravity-ease, mindlessly clean,
filtered and re-filtered through its own bed. *Water. Fall.*—

the good round taste of words in my mouth, solemnized
by graceful little silences. Actually, the words fall one by one
into an old lake of silence that right away I recognize
from when I used to grip the sides of the canoe in terror,

sliding over the lake with logs just beneath the surface,
seeing their sliminess and sinkingness that, at my age, felt
like a dream of death, or of my parents crumpling each other,
or their wrestling behind the door, hearing my mother, well—

yet another unspeakable sadness I couldn't stop,
and all the rest that later compressed like sedimentary rock
into my recurring dream of a buried body. Had I killed it?
I thought so. At least I buried it, I was guilty of that.

Rolled in a blanket under a dirt floor, it rotted slowly
as I tried out for cheerleader and failed, tried out
for marriage, succeeded and failed. Sometimes in the dream
I'd reveal the location. There would be an uncovering,

which would wake me up. And then the slow uncovering
of years, the therapists, the leaving, re-forming,
awakening. It's three o'clock, now. I'm awake, climbing,
grateful my body has lasted this long, proud of it for doing so,

of its muscular obedience. Of my whistling
"Delta Dawn" accurately, birdlike, into the wilderness,
What's that flower you have on? Could it be a faded rose
from days gone by? Which makes me think of "A Rose

for Emily" by William Faulkner, that master of the dust-mote,
of the winding down of families, of the last brave narrative
voice in a wilderness of silence, the grand and punitive
arrogance of thinking so, of dubbing any end the end.

And there I go again, hooking everything on everything
else, trying to get somewhere. *And did I hear you say,*
he was meetin' you here today, to take you to
his mansion in the sky? She's forty-nine, still waiting

in the song, still trying to get out of Brownville, crazy
with waiting or just plain crazy. The gnats are driving me crazy,
spots in front of my eyes, staying with me
as if my sweat were the last outpost of *eau-de-vie,*

as if I were the mansion. *In my Father's house are many mansions,*
repeated my Sunday school teacher, each one festooned,
cordoned off, a gem-facet of the great Truth
made up somehow of Christians, Muslims, Hindus,

Buddhists, Jews, that I would reach, I thought, I was not told,
still I thought, still I kept on uphill to take the SATs,
the GREs, read the Bible, work out, eat less cheese,
learn to maintain my boundaries, which is why,

in the first decade of the twenty-first century, I,
product of all that well-doing, am in love with Bridal Veil Falls,
gnats notwithstanding, with the upswell of undercurrent,
the well-marked Goal: the marriage of light-

spray to the speechless dark. However, having not exactly
planned this trip, having only two hours free,
and no water bottle—and the next couple I meet
says another hour up at least—I turn back, not without

hesitation, not without a slow turning and turning again,
a long look uphill, feet ready to go, but turning, the vibration
of my longing gradually easing itself into a hum, a rhythm,
an oddly comforting dissonance—I admit: an elation.

A poison-ivy-edged, gnat-worried, leaf-swaled, rock-ribbed
elation. I'm whistling. Something I love I won't have today.
It's spilling out beyond me and tumbling down,
and doesn't know the word "love" from Adam. I've found

a walking stick and three-leggedly thump the sharp decline,
in the sixty-first year of my life, the narrative line
disappearing into the earth, cool as snow-melt,
absence leaving a certain awe behind, and joy as its sign.

The Felix Pollak Prize in Poetry

Ronald Wallace, General Editor

Now We're Getting Somewhere · David Clewell
Henry Taylor, Judge, 1994

The Legend of Light · Bob Hicok
Carolyn Kizer, Judge, 1995

Fragments in Us: Recent and Earlier Poems · Dennis Trudell
Philip Levine, Judge, 1996

Don't Explain · Betsy Sholl
Rita Dove, Judge, 1997

Mrs. Dumpty · Chana Bloch
Donald Hall, Judge, 1998

Liver · Charles Harper Webb
Robert Bly, Judge, 1999

Ejo · Derick Burleson
Alicia Ostriker, Judge, 2000

Borrowed Dress · Cathy Colman
Mark Doty, Judge, 2001

Ripe · Roy Jacobstein
Edward Hirsch, Judge, 2002

The Year We Studied Women · Bruce Snider
Kelly Cherry, Judge, 2003

A Sail to Great Island · Alan Feldman
Carl Dennis, Judge, 2004

Funny · Jennifer Michael Hecht
Billy Collins, Judge, 2005

Reunion · Fleda Brown
Linda Gregerson, Judge, 2007